Time to Talk

First published in 2013 by Grass Roots Press

Grass Roots Press gratefully acknowledges the financial
support for its publishing programs provided by the
following agencies: the Government of Canada through
the Canada Book Fund and the Government of Alberta
through the Alberta Foundation for the Arts.

Alberta
Foundation
for the Arts

Library and Archives Canada Cataloguing in Publication

Reiff, Tana
        Time to talk / Tana Reiff. — Rev. ed.

(Pathfinders)
Previous title: Time to choose.
ISBN 978–1–927499–63–4

        1. Readers (Adult). 2. Readers for new literates.
I. Reiff, Tana. Time to choose. II. Title. III. Series:
Pathfinders (Edmonton, Alta.)

PE1126.A4R4475 2013   428.6'2   C2012–906772–5

Cover image: © Randy Faris/Corbis

Printed and bound in Canada.

Time to Talk

Tana Reiff

Grass Roots Press

Chapter 1

The car
was almost ready
for the Hot Summer race.
It would be
Bob's first time.
He had gone
to the races
for many years.
Now, at last,
he would be
driving in one.

Every day,
Bob went
right from his job
to the garage.
He worked and worked
on his car.
After each run
he found something else
to fix.

The car took time,
but it was fun.
All the work
would pay off.
if he won the race.

Between his job
and the car,
Bob saw very little
of his wife, Mia.
Their two girls
were in bed
when he got home
at night.
He almost never saw them.

A big chunk
of Bob's pay
went into the car.
Mia had needed
a new washer
for a long time.
She stopped
bringing it up.

Bob forgot about it.
Mia only hoped
that the washer
would not break down.

Bob just kept on
working on his car.
He loved to fine-tune it.
He loved to see it
shine in the sun.
He loved showing it off
to his friends
at the garage.
Most of all,
he loved driving it.
Bob knew he had
the best car
on the road.
He had made it
that way.
He was very proud.
But it cost
a lot of time
and money.

Chapter 2

The Hot Summer race
was only a week away.
Bob's car
was in good shape.
Bob was sure
he would do well
in this race.
He would
cross the finish line
in first place.

But every day
was a race against time.
So Bob started
calling in sick
to his job.
After three days
of calling in,
the boss stopped by
to talk to Bob.

He said,
"Okay, Bob.
Enough is enough.
We don't need you anymore.
You're out."

Bob could not believe
he had been fired.
But he had.

"I hated that job,"
he told Mia.
"No big deal.
This is a break!
Now I'll have time
to get the car just right.
And then I'll win
the Hot Summer race.
This is only the start!
I will be
a full-time driver!"

Mia did not
take the job news
so well.

"Bob," she said.
"You lost your job!
What are we going to do?
How can we live?"

Then, for the first time,
Mia told Bob
how she really felt.

"Don't you see
what that car is doing
to the kids and me?
We almost never
see you.
You're always working
on your car.
Or you're at the track."
Mia started to cry.
"So much money—
our money—
goes into the car.
The girls' clothes
are getting too small.

The washer
is on its last legs.
We have bills.
Where is the money
to live on
going to come from?"

"Don't worry,"
said Bob.
"You watch.
I'm going to win
the Hot Summer race.
And then
I'll win other races.
We are going to be rich!"

Mia wiped her eyes.
"Right," she said softly.

Bob did not hear her.
He was out the door,
off to the garage.

Chapter 3

It was the day
of the Hot Summer race.
Bob and the car
were ready to run.
Bob had not been
home very much
for the last week.
He stopped in
only to eat and sleep.

Mia and the girls
came to see Bob
in the big race.

Everything about the car
felt right.
It ran
like a dream.
Nothing could go wrong.
Bob was sure.

A loud voice
filled the air.
"Start your engines!"
All 30 cars
took a rolling start.
The green flag waved.
They were off.

Bob's car
dashed out
and took the early lead.
The car felt great.
Then two cars
passed him.
Bob pressed
the gas pedal
to the floor.
He passed
the two other cars.
Now he was
in front of the pack
again.
Bob's mind
was racing too.

I'm winning!
I'm winning!
I'm winning!
He looked ahead.
He could see no cars,
only track.
He drove faster.
And faster.
Nothing can stop me now!

And then, in a blink,
all was not right.
Bob could hear
the back tire blow out.
All of a sudden,
it was life or death.
Bob thought fast.
He took his foot
off the gas.
The car slowed down.
He could steer it now.

He got the car
off to the side
of the track.

Only then did he
let out his breath.
He was safe.
He had saved
his own life.

Those few seconds
had seemed like years.
Bob had never
used his head so well.

"They say
a good driver
knows how to act fast,"
he told Mia that night.
"I guess
I'm a pretty good driver."

"You're lucky
to be alive,"
Mia said.

"But, Mia,
I lost the race."

Mia put her arms
around him.
"Yes, Bobby,
you didn't win.
But you are alive.
Thank heavens!
You are alive
and not even hurt!
Do you know
how lucky we are?"

She looked
over his head
at the wall.
She wished she knew
how they would live.
There was no prize
from the race.
And no money
coming in either.

Chapter 4

Bob felt bad
about the Hot Summer race.
He spent
the whole next week
with the car.
Before anything else,
the car needed
a new set of tires.
The Fall Run
was coming up.
If he could
get the car ready,
he could win that race.
He just knew it.
But time was short.

Mia was not happy.
Even without a job,
Bob was not home much.
She kept her eye

on the money.
They had saved
for a time like this.
Now, the saved money
was going fast.

"Bob, we are running
out of money,"
she said one night.
"I'm scared.
You need
to find a job."

Bob's mind
was on the car,
not the bills.
He asked Mia,
"Why don't *you*
get a job?"

"My job
is to be here
for the kids,"
Mia said.

"That was the deal,
right?"

"It's different now,"
Bob said.
"The car
is going to make money
real soon.
Count on it.
You could
keep us going
if you found work."

Bob's last payday
had come and gone.
His mind was not
on finding a new job.
And so Mia
had no choice.
She had to find a job.

She found one
in a men's clothing store.
The girls

stayed with Mia's mother
while she worked.
And while Bob
worked on his car.

The bills sat and waited.
It would be two weeks
until Mia got paid.

Chapter 5

At the men's store,
Mia was on her feet
all day long.
The owner, Lou,
was easy to get along with.
Most of the customers
were friendly and nice.
Some were not.
Mia did her best
to please everyone.

After work,
Mia picked up the girls.
When she got home,
she was tired.
All she wanted to do
was put up her feet.
But she couldn't do
what she wanted.
She had to clean up the house
and make dinner.

And clean up after dinner.
Then make sure
the girls did their homework.
Then give the girls
a bath.
Then read them a story
and put them to bed.
After that,
Mia fell into bed herself.
By the end of the day,
there was nothing left
of her.

Bob shook her awake
when he came to bed.
"Have to get up early!"
he smiled.
"The car calls me!"

"Bob, please,"
said Mia.
"Please find a job.
Please?
I'm killing myself.
I need your help."

"I thought
you *liked* your job,"
said Bob.

"It's all right.
It's just too much.
I work all day.
Then I work all night
until I crash.
I don't have a minute
to do anything
that *I* want to do."

"Okay, okay."
Bob turned over in bed.
"Have it your way.
I'll sell the car.
I'll get a job.
But, Mia,
I'm so sure
I can make it.
Can't you try
to stick it out?"

Mia asked,
"Do you really think
you can win?"

"Of course, I do!
I really do.
And when I do,
I'll be the happiest guy
in the world."

Maybe you will,
Mia thought to herself.
But what about us?
What about this family?

"Okay," Mia said.
"I'll keep working.
But only until the Fall Run.
If you don't win
that race,
I'll quit my job
and you'll get a job."

"That's fair,"
Bob had to say.

"I'm sorry
I spend
so much time
with the car.
You know
I love you
and the girls.
I just have to do this.
I have to.
Now or never!
You only live once!
Life is short!
That's how I feel.
Can you see that?"

Mia said nothing.
She turned over
and went to sleep.

Chapter 6

The day
of the Fall Run
was beautiful.
The sun
shone like gold.
Bob took that
as a good sign
for the race.

In the morning,
Mia took the girls
to the park.
They played
on the swings.
They ran around.
All three of them.
When it was time
to go to the track,
they felt ready.

Bob felt ready too.
The car
looked so fine.
He felt sure
he could win today.
Win this race,
he thought,
and the day was his.
The prize money too.

His race
was the last
of the day.
He couldn't see
his family
in the stands.
But they were there.

He took his car
to the starting line.
"Start your engines!"
The green flag waved.
From a rolling start,
Bob shot out

like a rocket.
So did
the other cars.
They moved
in a tight pack
for half a lap
around the track.

Bob got out front.
Then another car
pulled ahead of him.
Bob passed him
and got a good lead.
He left
the other cars
in the dust.

Before he knew it,
the race was over.
He saw
the chequered flag
wave him
over the finish line.
He had won!

Mia and the girls
ran to meet Bob.
All four of them hugged
and jumped up and down.
Bob was the star
of the day.
Everyone crowded
around him
in the winner's circle.
The band
played music.
Everyone
talked at once.
Everyone
wanted to shake
Bob's hand.
And pat him on the back.
Someone poured beer
over his head.

Maybe Bob was right
after all,
Mia thought.
He said he would win,

and he did.
Maybe car racing
was what
he should be doing.

Chapter 7

Winning the Fall Run
was a big break
for Bob.
One good race
made him want
to win again.
So he still spent
all of his time
with the car.

Because Bob won
the race,
Mia kept her job.
One prize
would not pay the bills
for very long.
In fact,
most of the prize money
went back into the car.

Mia got very good
at selling men's clothes.
She did not love the job.
She just smiled
and sold more
than anyone else.

Lou, the owner,
never stopped
telling Mia
how good she was.
"You are so right
for this job!"
he told her.
"I want to take you
out to lunch!"

"Just me?"
Mia asked him.

"Just the two of us,"
Lou smiled.

He took Mia
to the best place in town.

He bought her
a drink.
He laughed
at her jokes.
He told her
how smart she was.
Bob had not
treated her like that
in years.
She was taken
with Lou.
He made her
feel good.
She began
to forget about
her problems at home.

One lunch
turned into a drink
every day after work.
Sometimes a drink
turned into dinner.
Mia knew
she did not have time
for this.

Something about this
did not feel right.
Some nights,
she asked her mother
to give the kids dinner.
She told her mother
she had to work late.

The girls began
to ask questions.
"Where's Mommy and Daddy?"
Mia's mother
would always say,
"They are very busy, kittens.
They will kiss you good night
when they get home."

As the girls
were going to bed,
their mother
was with Lou.

"I really like you,"
Lou was telling Mia.
"It's too bad

you're married.
We could be
close friends."

Mia didn't know
what to say.
She knew
she was married
with two children.
But Lou—
well, he was
another world.
A world she liked.

Lou went on.
"Your husband
doesn't spend much time
at home,
does he?"

"No," said Mia.
"He races a car.
He works on the car.
He tests it
on the track.

He is sure
it will all pay off."

Lou said,
"So you work
while he plays
with his car?"

Mia looked down.
"You could say that.
But I'm starting
to like work more."
She looked up.
"You tell me
I'm good at it."

Lou asked
another question.
"Have you ever thought
about leaving your husband?"

"Not really,"
said Mia.
"Until now."

Chapter 8

One day at the store,
Lou took Mia aside.

"I have something
to ask you,"
he began.
"I know a place
on a lake.
Can you get away
for the weekend?
I want us
to get to know
each other
much better."

"For the weekend?"
Mia asked.
"I don't know.
What would I tell
my husband
and the children?"

"Tell them
you are going
to a sales meeting,"
Lou said.

Mia thought
about Lou's idea
for a few minutes.
Go away with Lou?
That would be
a big step.
She wasn't sure
she should do that.
It wouldn't be fair
to Bob.
On the other hand,
was Bob being fair
to her?
She could think
of nothing nicer
than a weekend
with Lou.

"Yes," she said.
"I'd like to go.

I'll work it out."

After work Friday,
Lou and Mia
drove to the lake.
They had
a quiet dinner
with wine and candles.
After dinner,
they sat on the grass
and looked up
at the stars.
The sky was clear.
A million stars
lit the night.
They talked
about many things—
about growing up,
about their school days,
about their families,
about themselves.

On Saturday
they visited
the famous gardens

by the lake.
They walked
in fields of flowers.
They walked a path
through the woods.
They held hands.

By breakfast
on Sunday,
Mia and Lou
were more than friends.
They had learned
so much
about each other.
Mia had learned
about herself too.

After breakfast,
they took
one last walk.
The lake was still.
The air was cool.
Mia was quiet.

"Have you had
a good time
this weekend?"
Lou asked.

"I have,"
Mia smiled.

"Are you glad
you came here
with me?"
Lou asked.

"It's another world,"
Mia said.
She looked Lou
in the eye.
"But you know what?
It's not
the real world.
It's too good
to be real."

"What do you mean?"
Lou wanted to know.
"Something can be
good and real
at the same time."

"I like you a lot, Lou,"
Mia went on.
"But we can't do this
ever again.
I'm sorry.
I must face
my real world
at home."

Lou said nothing.
He knew Mia
better now.
He knew now
that she could not
toss away her life.
Not for him,
and not for a good time.

Driving home,
Lou began to talk.
"Mia, this has been
a beautiful weekend.
You've been
so good to me.
And I hope
I've been good
to you.
But I get it.
I get you.
You must go back
and deal with
your real world.
I will not
get in your way."

Mia took his hand.
All she could say was
"Thank you, Lou."

She brushed
a little tear
from her face.

Then she looked
at the road ahead.
It was long,
with many twists and
turns.
But it would
take her home,
where she knew
she must go.

Chapter 9

The Friday that Mia left
for the lake,
Bob came home early.
He had been thinking.
Maybe Mia
was right.
Maybe he did
spend too much time
with the car.
Maybe he did
need to be home more.
So he came home
to help out.
He wanted
to show Mia
where his heart was.

Dishes were in a pile
in the sink.
Bob washed them.

He swept
the whole house.
He even washed
some clothes.

By the time it got dark,
Mia and the girls
still weren't home.
So Bob called
Mia's mother.

"She had to go
out of town,"
said Mia's mother.
"A sales meeting,
I think she said.
She'll be back
on Sunday.
I have the girls here.
So the weekend
is all yours
to work on your car."

"Okay, thanks,"
was all he said.

A sales meeting?
Since when
does the store
have sales meetings
out of town?
Why didn't Mia tell him
she was going away?
Something was off.

At dinnertime
on Sunday,
Mia came home.

"Hello, Bob,"
she said,
without a hello kiss.
There was ice
in her voice.
She called him Bob,
not Bobby.
"Are the girls
still with my mother?"

"Yes," Bob said.
"I'll pick them up.

But why didn't you
tell me sooner
that you were going away?
Where have you been?"

"You don't seem to care
what I'm doing,"
said Mia.
"I wasn't sure
you would even see
that I was gone."

"Really?
Is that so?
It might surprise you
to know
that I came home
early Friday.
I cleaned up
around the house.
Did all kinds of stuff
around here."

"Nice," said Mia.
"Too little, too late.
But nice of you."

"Too late, Mia?
I came home Friday
because I
haven't been fair to you."

"You're right,"
said Mia.
"You haven't been fair."

Bob moved close
to Mia.
He reached out
for her hands.
Slowly,
Mia put out her hands
and took hold of his.

"You know what?"
said Mia,
"I haven't been
fair to you either.

I should have told you
that I was going away.
Or not go at all."

"Bobby," said Mia.
"Let's make up our minds
right here and now.
Both of us.
Let's promise
to always be fair
to each other.
No matter what.
Are you with me, Bobby?"

Bob let go
of Mia's hands.
He put his arms
around her
and held her tight.
"I'm with you,"
he said.

Mia moved
her head back

and looked Bob
in the face.
"You don't think
car racing
will come between us
ever again?"

"I won't let it,"
Bob promised.
"I want to race.
But I choose you
over the car.
Nothing makes me
feel like a winner
more than
our life together."

Chapter 10

Mia quit her job
at the men's store.
She loved the way
Lou made her feel.
But she couldn't work
with him anymore.
She found a new job
in an office.

Bob never knew
why Mia changed jobs.
She would never
tell him why.

But what about
the money?
They were living
hand to mouth.
They were cutting down
in every way
to save money.

Mia did not like
living like this.

Winter was
on the way.
Bob was already getting
his car in shape
for the first spring race.
One day
Mia called him
while he was working
on the car.

"Do you know
someone named Joe Silva?"
she asked.
"He wants to talk to you
about a job."

"A job?
The car *is* my job,"
said Bob.
"We'll be fine
if I keep on winning."

"Yes, Bob,"
said Mia.
"If you keep on winning.
But what if you don't?"

"Every race
is a new chance!"
said Bob.

"Every race
is a new risk too,"
said Mia.
"This could be
a long, hard winter.
Please call Joe.
This could be
just what we need.
Please?"

"Okay, okay.
I'll call
and find out
what's up."

"Thanks, Bobby,"
said Mia.
"Let me know
what Joe says."

Chapter 11

Joe and Bob
had been friends
for a long time.
Joe ran
a big garage in town.
He could fix
any car
and do a fine job.

"Hey, Joe!"
said Bob on the phone.
"What's up?"

"Hey, Bob!
I need
a new head mechanic,"
said Joe.
"I need the best,
and you're the best.
I know you're

busy with your race car.
But I want you
to work for me.
What do you say?"

Bob said nothing.

Joe waited.
Still no answer from Bob.

At last,
Joe began to speak.
"I need you, Bob.
Full time.
Good pay.
How about it?"

"Boy, Joe,
I don't know.
I've been spending
most of my time
with my car.
I haven't been thinking
about a full-time job."

"Think it over, Bob,"
Joe said.
"This job
is a sure thing.
Racing your car
is taking big chances."

"I'll think about it,"
said Bob.
I'll call you
in the morning."

"You're good,"
Joe added.
"You're a good driver
and a good mechanic.
You can do both
and make everyone happy.
You can work it out."

Chapter 12

Bob was on his back
under the car.
He spotted
a brown-orange line
on a pipe.
I baby this car,
he thought.
How in the world
did rust
get on there?
He scraped it off.
Then he touched it up
with car soap.
He let it dry.

The whole time,
he was thinking.
No way
did he want
to give up racing.

He loved it.
He lived for it.
He had worked so hard.
And he was winning.

But what if
he didn't keep on winning?
He had never let himself
think he wouldn't win.

He had to
make some money.
He had to be fair
to Mia and the girls.
He had promised
to be fair.

Could he really
work full-time
and keep racing?
Could he do both
without going crazy?
Could he
spend less time
with the car

and still win races?
Would he
see his family
any less
than he already did?

So many questions.
Things didn't add up.
He had no answer.

Just then,
Bob heard a knock
on the car hood.
"Who's there?"
he called
as he slid out
from under the car.

"Name is Tom Ross.
Are you the guy
who drives this car?
Or the mechanic?"

"I'm both,"
said Bob.

"I do it all."
He laughed.

"I saw you race
in the Fall Run,"
Tom went on.
"You have
no stickers
on your car.
You have
no sponsors?"

"No, not yet,"
said Bob.
"Haven't had time
to go after a sponsor."

"Well, I might be
a sponsor
going after *you*!"
Tom said.

"What? Really?
Sponsor my car?"

What a break!
Someone wanted
to pay for ad space
on the car!
Bob's mind was racing,
just like his car
on the track.
He could even pay
a mechanic
to help him out.

"The more you win,
the more I can give,"
Tom said.

Bob wiped himself off
and shook Tom's hand.
"Let's talk about this!"
he said.

Joe Silva
and the job in town
were wiped
from Bob's mind.

Chapter 13

"Mia!" Bob called
as he ran
into the house.
"Wait till you hear this!
A man named Tom Ross
wants to sponsor
my car!
We're set!
This is it!"

Mia gave him
a little smile.
"That's nice,"
she said.
"And what did
Joe Silva
have to say?"

"Oh," said Bob.
"He wants

to give me a job
as head mechanic.
But, Mia, who needs that
when I can race
and not think
about the money?"

"Bobby, we both know
it's not that easy,"
Mia said.
"There is
a lot more to it
than that.
Have you
made up your mind
or can we talk
about it?"

Bob's mouth
was going up and down.
But no words
were coming out.
Everything had been
so clear to him

until he talked
to Mia.

"Number one,"
Mia began,
"you might need
more than one sponsor.
Number two,
with enough sponsors,
you could hire
a part-time mechanic.
That would free you
to take the job."

Now Bob spoke.
"I did think
about getting some help.
That would give me
more time at home.
I hadn't thought
about having time
for a job."

"The girls
are at my mother's.
Let's go out
to dinner, Bobby,"
said Mia.
"Let's talk about this."

"Dinner costs money,"
Bob said.

"Okay, let's make
some sandwiches,"
said Mia.
"We can take them
to the park
and talk."

"Let's go,"
said Bob.
"I can't
think this out
by myself.
Two heads
are better than one!"

"Bobby, we will
work this out,"
said Mia.
"The two of us
will work this out.
Together."

Bob opened the door.
Out they stepped
into the fresh air.
Together.